The Poet's Wife Speaks

by Mary Ellen Miller

D1418109

OLD SEVENTY CREEK PRESS POETRY PRIZE 2011

OLD SEVENTY CREEK PRESS POETRY SERIES 2011

COPYRIGHT 2011 BY RUDY THOMAS

2011 OLD SEVENTY CREEK FIRST EDITION
PRINTED IN THE UNITED STATES OF AMERICA
ALL RIGHTS RESERVED UNDER INTERNATIONAL
AND PAN-AMERICAN COPYRIGHT CONVENTIONS

PUBLISHED IN THE UNITED STATES
BY OLD SEVENTY CREEK PRESS
RUDY THOMAS, PUBLISHER
P. O. BOX 204
ALBANY, KENTUCKY 42602

ISBN-13: 978-1463641108
ISBN-10: 1463641109

PRINTED BY CREATE SPACE FOR
OLD SEVENTY CREEK PRESS

Dedicated

To

Morgan Eklund
and
Jane Olmsted

with gratitude for their love and inspiration.

And, as with everything,
For
Jim Wayne Miller

and our children
Jim, Fred, Ruth

Acknowledgments

"Arrival" Plainsong. Vol IV. No. 1. Spring 1982.

"Choices." Plainsong. Vol I. No. 2. Fall, 1979

"Things in the Shape of Other Things." *Writing Who We Are: Poems by Kentucky Feminists*. Western Kentucky University: 1999.

"Reading Your Poems." Appalachian Heritage. Vol. 5. No 3. Summer, 1977.

"The Feet of the Messenger." Plainsong. Vol 1. No. 2. Fall, 1979.

"The Poet's Wife Speaks." Adena. Vol. 4. No. 1. Spring, 1979.

"Stepmother." *Writing Who We Are: Poems by Kentucky Feminists*. Western Kentucky University: 1999.

"The Orchard." *Appalachian Heritage*. Vol. 5. No. 3. Summer, 1977.

"The Combination." *South*. Vol. 5. No. 2. Spring 1973.

"Tongue-tied." *The Journal of Kentucky Studies*. Vol. 7. September, 1990.

"The Party." *The* Writer. July 1965.

"What Did You See?" *The Journal of Appalachian Studies.* Vol. 7. September, 1990.

"Better Closing Lines." *Appalachian Heritage.* Vol 28. No. 1. Winter, 2000.

Special thanks to my granddaughter, Marietta J. Miller, for the cover illustration, "The Green Coat," a hand-drawn monoprint.

Introduction

Biting into these crisp, delicious poems is like biting into a fresh hard apple: the sweetness is intensified by sharpness. Here is the fruit of wisdom, hard-won.

Wit and charm sparkle throughout: speaking of metaphors, "Pie works as well as sky, if you think about it." "The middle of things is where the juices are." Pork roast, butterscotch pies, death, tears—the harvest of the poet's life—defined in the end not by her wifedom but by her gift—flourishes on the tree of her craft. It is not for nothing that in "The cat strolled in brandishing a rabbit" there is no comma; this is strolling itself, uninterrupted.

Wisdom, hard won but not hard, always knows its limit and keeps its secret smile: "I have found/Nothing matters at all, /Unless it's old and done in orderly fashion." The poet knows she has become, in spite of herself, the "Pillar" of her community, the one depended on—as so many women are—to cook cookies for the school and organize the meetings; but she is a pillar rooted not in these obligations but in the deep loam of her poetry.

Finally, there is Miller's deep connection with other writers, with the whole rich field of women's accomplishment. Her book is a celebration of the spirit that thrives on what we view as ordinary and survives what we think cannot be survived, with panache, with hope, with grace.

Sallie Bingham, Fiction Writer, Poet, Playwright, Teacher, Feminist Activist

For Mary Ellen Miller
A Poem by Morgan Eklund

Women of the Poets

are poets too—
executives of the estates,
the papers,
the written bloods—
recorded guilt,
from warm seasons
that cannot stay under
foliage, soil.

In the morning
the women and words left behind
carry around the broken bread bodies
of the poet men,
to make sure
their hands are still
read— deep in the cove
beside a fireplace.

We want so much
for them to be remembered
like glass remembers
water molecules clumped.
Like we remember. . .
all things the poets
bred, whispered
from their eyes—
the escape
that told us what land
they were from.

The Poet's Wife Speaks

The Poet's Wife Speaks

Welcome home, Darling,
        while you were gone,
        I invented you.

The money is in the refrigerator.
The children are folded in their drawers.
I ironed the dog and cats.

There were no calls.

The house took sick
        while you were gone
        I had to call someone in to spray.

Now don't let it depress you.

They aren't sure what—
        some kind of fungus
        got started in your clothes
        and spread to your briefcase
        and thence all over the house.

I was looking for a poem when I first noticed the smell.

I said to myself:
        if I put the money in the refrigerator
        where would you put a poem?

You would put it with your grandfather because he is
already dead.

I remembered his name immediately because it
wasn't the same as mine which I forgot.

Before you go to sleep will you check for me? I
think I hid under the bed.

1

They say the house will have to go;

There's a condemned sign on the front door.

Will you cut up the furniture for dinner?
I am all tied up under the bed.

Somebody wrote a poem about me
        and buried it under
        his grandfather's name.

I have to take a walk now.

They are calling my name in the street outside.
They want me to come out and play.

Will you look with me?
        I'm here somewhere under the bed
        or I may have gone to the attic
        to take a dip in the pool.

Darn it. I just can't keep up with anything.

Oh, did I tell you the mailman came by
        and I gave him a bath
        in your name?

He said that way I could take it off the tax.

This Poem

This poem is going to happen
in its own sweet time.

It decided all by itself
not to hurry.

The sky is falling;
the sky is falling.

Slowly and surely
its kind, round shoulders
hugging the world.

This poem is a child
dragging an arm through a sweater.
It says, "There's time.
Plenty of time."

Time is the slowest thing on earth.
Except this poem

which is a slug
leaking ribbons of silver
going nowhere in pieces of eight.

Red

First I took the cookies
down the hill to Grandma's house.

Then ran and ran—
time was so precious.

He was there!
His eyes red with lust
and sleeplessness—

Just hands and tongue
too young, too young,
he always told me.

My woodsman!
Naked in his arms
I tried to hold him

but angry villagers
who heard me
crying joy,
crying glory

chopped off his head
and then the myth began:

> A big bad wolf ate my old granny
> (Idiots! She's still alive.)
> and tried to force me to his bed.

At night I eat my metaphors
and wipe my mouth with similes.
My naughty parts glow in the dark.
My tiny breasts—electrified—flash:
HOLD ME! HOLD ME!
The last words he ever said.

4

Cote d' Azur

There's a poster on the wall my daughter mailed
blue of sky-and-water field
from the land of loveliness.

Dormir sous un saphir.

Black words like creatures crawling on the blue.

Between the blues a young girl sleeps.

"Because the colors are so wonderful,
because the earth is elsewhere dirty,
you should post it on the wall."

Now. . . thinking of a girl my daughter's age
who swam into your life
I see the poster daily
thinking blue and rock firm thighs
and sapphire seas and her eyes
blue as the poster blue,
saying to myself:

I will not die on this thought

and buying flowers for my daughter's room
to celebrate her sky-and-water body
and her eyes.

Also, the other's eyes.

Arrival

Here comes my poem
It gallops up wet
Foaming at the mouth
Saddled, bridled
Out of breath.

I ride the last ounce
Of its energy

Deep into the landscape
Shaped like a keyhole
Dipping down, down
Horse and rider
We fade into the sage.

Desire

The June breeze will tell you:
the middle of things is where the juices are;
where the years bulge best with desire
though nothing worth desire can be defined—
I have known this so long and wanted to tell you.

You are the servant of something about to happen.
You were never meant to be young—a dreadful mistake
on the verge of correction.

I am only your carpet, your coat, a soft pillow,
a good place to file—those things you miss only
in their absence, like teeth, like water.

When your heart has that afternoon hurt,
breathe deeply the comfort from those you have harmed.
We have all failed in all things that matter
and excuse ourselves even better than gods.

Think of clean nights under the stars,
the way light startles the water,
other beds and hair dark on the pillow,
 of what I am like with another
his hand massaging my heart,
how dangerous I am loving you better
and rocks rinsed by waves
on shores where cranes wade at dawn.

No Place to Hide

There are still too many suns to run on this city.
This place.
Cold with its warm lights.
Night without stars.
This place. This place.

I sit in my chair.
They say another ice age is coming.
I am already worried.
Big cakes of it will rain from the sky,
taking everyone but me by surprise.
I will have time. . .
time to do what?
Crawl under my chair and say,
"Look out. It's coming."

A Poem for Readers of Poems

All bundled up in leftover wrappings
of all my hours and yours*
stale but warm to sleep and dream
            (*meaning yours and yours and yours).

Now I have to go to the bathroom.

WARNING: this is the story of my life.

I have found:
            Nothing matters at all,
            unless it's old and done in orderly fashion.

Cave drawings are carved on my skull.
There's a list in the files:
            first, antelope
            then, the bison.

I warned you and you kept on reading.

Now you know why—some of the time—
I love the world and all that's in it.

But mostly I love you—
patient, forgiving—
who start and end
wishing me well.

Ask Me

(A poem for English Majors)

Ask me: lines that I have learned
that caught the sun in flight
and burned into my brain
like raisins in a bun
or small frogs flattened on the road
where three forks meet
and some space shines like leveled lakes
I might be walking on.

Ask me: how we can know
the dancer from the dance;
a jar in Tennessee completely bare
from fancy urns with maidens fair;
or men who strove with gods
far on the windy plains from Troy
Donahue. Ask me.

I sit upon a bough and sing
of coffee spoons that measure out
our lives and circus lady moons
Where all is accustomed, born, and dies
and no one sees or has the right,
not yet, before they leap into the light.

Ask me: who walks in beauty
or has a heart too soon made glad
or hates the narrow glide of snakes
enough to toss them like a rind—

Ask me. I have been her kind.

But hurry up please,
It's time.

Or ask: What is the grass?
I will listen. It is Kleenex for the lord
and full of godly snot. No splendor there.

10

And here's another fuss:
the woods are lovely, dark, but cheap
and I like gold to airy thinness beat
and not a bodily thing
though bobolinks for choristers
and orchards where they sing
heard melodies so sweet
but not as sweet as those unheard
some say. Don't ask me why—
I grant I never heard an unheard song
or saw a goddess go.

But I have watched the snow
falling fast, oh, fast, but long enough
to say: It's all I know on earth
and nothing white can stay.

Choices

I had never walked barefoot
            on sandstone
And so. . . I think. . .
I decided to do it.

Or the act decided itself.

What should I have done?
We are all so full of our frost-rimmed holes
The rims steam if we blow on them

But they do not melt
            not even from the sun-warmed sandstone

Listen:

            A robin came down the chimney
            of my house and flew over my face.
            At 1:45 a.m. I knew it didn't
            mean anything. . . less at least
            then deciding to walk barefoot
                        on sandstone.

What if we stop pretending?
Would the earth close up
Like a woolly worm?
And toss us over the edge?
Or would I know what
Whoever said
            if we miss the physical world
            we have missed everything

Meant by it?

Whatever.

I would not put on my shoes
Or invent superstitions about robins

12

Coming down the chimney at 1:45.

Not even if it had been two—
two exactly and just as the
Town clock struck.

I am not afraid of robins.

Only of choices—
Walking on sandstone—
When the clear, neat path
Circles the grainy mass.
Loud and definitive.
And far more insistent than robins.

You Were Sleeping When it Happened

The cat strolled in brandishing a rabbit,
small and semi-eaten but still alive.
I screamed—not loud enough to wake you.
It was a muted scream, more a grinding
of some unused muscle in my throat.
(Listening back, the sound amazes.)
That awful moment, knowing as I did,
what must be done.

There's a towel in the garbage can outside.
It wraps a tiny, tiny heart still beating.

Your wife is in the shower, running the water
hot until it hurts. She hopes that dreadful business
in the towel will soon be done.

One time my careful car crushed a creature,
a darting, careless, well-dressed dog.
Back and forth I drove to polish off the job.
There was that heavy, cold machine between us.
Besides it was a matter of good manners.
I mashed that lump until the wheels ran flat.

Then I wrapped my work in my best coat
and bore it like a soldier
house to house until I found
the proper door.

True, this time I had no weapon
and you <u>were</u> sleeping when it happened.
Not to excuse myself (I am no warrior),
but, without some shield, I'll take the easy route.

As I Recall

There was no breeze—no breeze at all—
the day felt late and like a mild November.

But it was June, certifiably so,
Not that it matters.

I carried my heart in an old cat dish,
trailing IV lines behind me. . . .
Walking.

Memories—oh, long before that—
included summer sun and ripe peaches.

All kinds of trees and hands.
There were hands worthy of mention.

But memories decay—the good and the bad.
Peaches rot. They grow maggots.

I find that cataclysmic as death
or bad breath in a lover.

Still that sun, then and now,
warms my cool bones.

The honeysuckle suckles or whatever it does.
I think it rambles.

Summer purrs like a cat.
A cat that loves best its own dish.

The warmth of the sun
and the feel of one hand stroking.

Setting the Record Straight

There were three of everything—
they got that right—
but I was older than the tale implies,
old enough to worry Papa,

"Where you been, Goldie Girl?"

"Oh, just picking berries and wandered off the path."

And it was consommé, not porridge
light as wind and spiced with curry,
served in dainty pewter mugs.

Three chairs. Those chairs!
There's been no justice to the chairs.
Rockers with the softest padding,
brocade padding brilliant red.
When rocked, they played a lullaby.

It was right, I tell you.
It was just right.

And the beds, all in one room but what a room!
Big as a meadow
with windows everywhere.
Such light and lightness in those covers,
goose down I would guess
under crocheted lace white
white as home churned butter
like something in a fairy tale.

I stretched and arched and purred my favorite hymm,

"I saw the light; I saw the light."

And there they found me
sleeping sweetly, sleeping soundly.

16

"Oh, just picking berries and wandered off the path."

But I've lived uneasily ever after
and made a royal mess of things.
I've sent two husbands packing
from my clumsy jill and jacking.

I could never do what I was told.

Nothing here is really pretty
not even clean, just dark and dreary
and the corners of my life are furry,
fuzzy, dark and dank, dark and dirty.
There is dust in every nook and cranny of my brain.

I cannot keep clean.

But though the memory's blurry,
those beds were soft and furry,
and there was order, light and order,
radiance almost other-worldy,
like an anthem sweet and pearly—
oh hark the herald—soft and curly
that floats forever in my mind.

It was right, I tell you.
It was just right.

Traffic

(Stopped in traffic in my small town for the funeral procession of a
teenage boy killed in an accident after he left a drinking party.)

None of you stopped him
though you, my son,
told me next day
how hard you tried.

Especially his one best friend
who hid his keys
until he ripped the house apart
finally did give in
but followed after in his car
only to see the body
not sixty feet beyond the party house
shot like a paper wad
hard and quick and thin.

He didn't call officials.
Someone did
but ran his way
feeling faster than his car
back to the party
crying in,
"He's gone. I knew it."

How you had to deal with him
slobbering on the floor
saying over and over,
"I told him."

Dealt with him
before the party crowd
walked out to see
the lights of many circled cars.
And all so quickly done
before they rang the bell
(must have rung the bell),

18

"Mrs. Smith?"

The woman always hearing sooner
though he is fairly quick behind
"Huh, Honey? What? Who is it?"

Here at the traffic light
the suited policemen
even fat they look so trim
the flag-marked cars.

Teenagers who have shined their cars
sober little soldiers with their hair slicked back
faces dark with manly meaning
driving slowly with their racing thoughts.

19

Watching You Fish on Father's Day

Today, I will follow you to the ends of the earth
and knowing you, you will take me there.

What could I do that you would sit so patiently and watch?

It doesn't matter.
Here in your blue world of sky and water
I will love you more than you love me without regret.

I improve the time: texture of rock and sand.
Nature up close is full of holes.

Father's Day.
Daddy, we should have sent them to obedience school
and rubbed their noses in whatever they befouled.

Here you are boss.
Boss of the crickets,
"Hold still, fella,"
Lord of the fishing flies.

For this one day
I take my stand:
I will think and breathe and feel your world.
It is my way of making up
for not being simple enough to suit my man.

Are you wishing she, not I, were here?
It doesn't matter.
Here in this wet world of mud and water
I love you as you are:
Boss of the crickets.
Boss of the fish,
The trees, the sky, the sand.

20

Notecard

The sun lay sweet
on my face
mildly warm
and just plain lovely.
The starlings played
with the mulberry trees
in my backyard.
I was alone
as I always am
When nice things happen.

You know how you do
sometimes—just feeling
here it is right now
like you've hit the
first level of Zen
or just suddenly know
like those postcards say
that the Hokey Pokey
really is
what it's all about?

An Old-Fashioned Christmas

It's Christmas.
Yes, I waken early in this house
where all I love lie sleeping.

I must rise soon and light the fire.
I check my mental list
knowing already I have done those things
all mothers do for comfort and festivity.

In yonder room you sleep—fully clothed
on couch or chair, shunning my bed
for noise all night long.
I hear it now: selling salad spinners, hope, and pearls.

I'm satisfied I've kept on schedule here.

My sweet ones—long since grown—
their arms around their mates,
back in their old rooms.
Dear God, I love them so.
My in-law children almost more for daring
to adore, to cherish my imperfect angels.

There is something to be said for this.

And you? (I want to call you thee).
Dreaming perhaps of those whose lives you hulled like walnuts,
ate the meat, and kept the shells like ornaments for trees.
What unsuspecting goddess flies now in your dreams?
What radiant sky is cushion to your flight?

Something is missing here.

22

And, yet, the morning air is calm and clean.
I want to don my gay apparel and think old-fashioned thoughts:
There's mistletoe and holly in this house.

And dreams.

I wish you joy of dreams
this holy day
I want the manger warm,
the shepherds kind,
and wise men everywhere
to share their wisdom with us all.

23

That House

That house.
We ate severity every night for supper,
right after my father barked grace.
Nobody talked!

I was afraid in that house—
silence reminds me.

You understand: nobody told me anything—
oh, a few bloated lies
and mindless mottoes for living.

I am not afraid now
except that I fear I will die
before I have one boisterous thought
for a hand-me-down.

That house.
Only the flowers spoke—
in pots and jars all over the place.
Mother's flowers.
Growing here, growing there,
Overflowing everywhere.

Frivolous upstarts in their jubilant colors.
Mindless excess, full of themselves,
hearing their own grace,
obeying their own orders.

Beginnings

You will wake one morning
to a mirror message
        that last band-aid of hair
        stayed behind you on the pillow

On this morning
you will
        brush half a tooth
        down the drain

just as your wife announces
        today I have decided
        to enter the menopause

your son. . .
        the one. . .
            to be counted on. . .
will call to say
        I've dropped out of school
        and joined a commune.

He calls to give you
his new name
        Brother Sun Always Rising

Before you're uniformed for work
your daughter says
she's not going back to school
        not ever, ever going back
        I'm pregnant can't you understand?

All. . . all
        before the call. . .
            from the police station.

As you unwad secret bills
diarrhea insults your dog
who finds your shoe.

This is a beginning.
Treat it with respect.
        Laugh into the mirror
        at your new face.
Learn to smile
from the other side
of your mouth.
Practice it now.
It's easier than you thought.

This is a beginning.
Only you can write its end.
        anytime. . .
                anyway. . .
                        any end you want.

Pillar

I never wanted to be
a pillar of the community
or a pillar of anything else
for that matter.
Pillow, maybe,
a soft pillow for nice people
to rest on
but pillar?

Children force you into that—
before you know it
you're taking your turn.
There's the carpool
and the Valentine cookies
and the team snacks,
and it turns out you shine
here in two or three places—
especially the Valentine cookies
you bought plain at Kroger's
and fancied up with canned frosting
splashed with red hots and
Voila! You're a genius.
Your friend standing by,
disheartened and humiliated
by her drab-looking but delectable
and very expensive to make
Polish grandmother's date nut bars.

It starts that way—
little things. Someone is needed
to head the parents' school curriculum council
and several people remembering your glorious
Valentine cookies put your name forward and
you can't say No and shame your kids
by being uncooperative.

27

No, you're sunk.
And this chairship leads to heading
the fund drive for little Joshua
and his malfunctioning lungs
and a few more important chores.
Who can deny the importance?
and then it dawns on you.
It happened and you are a pillar.

But you are a pillar who reads *The London Review*
of Books and asks herself how Stephen Burt
(however talented) got to be such a favorite with them.
I met him once—charming man, gifted poet,
nibbling on the cheese straws
I made for his post-reading reception.
He said, "I understand you made these."
And I said Yes because he obviously enjoyed them.
But I never got around to telling him how much
 I loved his poetry because I could tell from the way
he caught the crumbs in his napkin and ate
those as well that he wouldn't have cared
a great deal about hearing that from someone
he had probably already labeled a pillar,
nice and good to have around
for occasions like this but still
a pillar.
It ends that way.

Things in the Shape of Other Things

Heart-shaped rugs
Bookend hands
Santa Claus banks
Elephant mugs.

I don't like that.

This thing in me
Shaped like a cat
Poised for attack
Hissing, back
Arched, tail
Up

I don't like that.

Reading Your Poems

That's all right—

       I mean the way
       the clank of the washing machine
       leftover life on the dining table
       multiple beeps and whines of the house

beat in your poems like a pulse.

You go to sleep in stale arms
of smoke in a bed of paper fodder.

And wake to notes and books
due at school yesterday.

The kids and I: our breath kills flies.
The click of our boots frightens
mice out of the house forever.

Only your dreams
you say in one way or another
       bear still the wonder of frost
       in the light of the stars
       hounds barking
       waist-deep in cold water.

You sit with us a stranger still cold from the hunt.
Your own eyes look at you from the faces of your
       children—
full of tangled thoughts.

My hands shake sorting the socks.

It's all right.

30

I move like an old film
jerky and dated and funny
in you though you and beyond
walking the future.

At night we turn you over in your sleep—
three little elves and big mama
working quietly together
the smallest slithers under furniture to retrieve your socks.

We huddle without sounds, happy
 the four of us together.

The glow of our faces
lights the dark cave of your open mouth.

A small girl pats your naked thigh.
We have stopped your snoring—
odd roars over your dreams of wild honey
in a mountain pasture.

I fold the cover over your hills
of bone and muscle.

Row after row of neat black hair
on your legs and chest
wave like spring grass in the future
dreams of my children.

What I want is mine.

I also know it is the dream that matters.

Sideswiped

Now hours have passed.
It is the feast of St. Valentine.
My fragility is hard in my mind.
The door handle in my left side
presses against me.
My headlights glow, old and wise.
My head in its case of glass
shimmers in the sunlight.
All about me I smell
the noise of life.
I stand today inside
the news of my death
hearing it happen.
Yesterday was a good day to die.
But I shine today
in my glass temple full of old festival
red paper hearts
banquets of candy.

Early Light

Did I tell you
that time
my brother found
his sweet baby chicks
colorfully strewn by
an overnight fox
who killed and killed
way past his hunger
and how my brother
howled and howled
and how after
that he never gave
much of a shit
about anything?

That was why,
we said among
ourselves, he
served in the
Korean War
with such impeccable
manners: he had
already hurt all he could
by the dawn's early light
and why, even now,
he lives in a forest
still as the morning
sun on little triangular
feet or on the ramparts
he watched in such
soldierly silence.

No.
I never told you.

Did I mention
that morning I stopped
in a field
on my grandfather's farm
because the light caught
in my throat
like a swallowed sob—
the shine on the hay
the feel of October,
the sense that my life
shone before me with
indescribable promise.
My first grown-up event
in light on silence.

No.
I never told you.

Now, it's too late
but it always was
and here I am—
at my age—
in my own perilous night
needing something more,
something else to so proudly hail,
to hush my mouth and teach me
respect for the examples
above and all other
systems of silence.

An Imaginary Conversation with Mondrian

I say, "The moon may be square for all I know,
but did you know lab rats left alone
give themselves shocks for something to do?
That dust bunnies eat and excrete?
We suck their tiny poops like lollipops.
Jeff Chandler was a cross dresser?"

"Look," he says, "I have my own list of horrors.
I have measured the immeasurable world
and found nothing to love but sharp edges,
bold colors, the foxtrot, and my wooden tulip.
I have boxed the world in a frame suited
for framing. And what have you done?"

I say, "What is that noise at the window?"
Is it Himself come back to kill me?
I was ruined by love.
Oh, enough already."

He says, "I redeem myself. My workshop
is one of redemption. There are little squares
with big square ambitions. I never found
the shape of meaning, so I shaped it myself."

"But are dwarfed trees beautiful? Bound feet?
How far are you willing to go? Help me here."

I think he has gone to bed.

So here I am before "Composition London"—
I, who had looked under rocks for recompense
for the uneven world, now stand like a wind-
rocked boat righting itself to an insistent
and perhaps even holy equilibrium.

35

The Feet of the Messenger

          were encased in huge marshmallows;
Her voice had been wrapped in wool
          and kept under water.

It's been five minutes now, she hummed,
          since last she breathed.

I had to tell my sister that meant that she was dead.
Dying is such soft business in intensive care.

I had looked at her body while the chest still heaved—
          fragile as a pencil point—
          the split bones sacked in their case of skin.

I said things to her inside my head:
hang on, Mother, you'll make it, Mother.
I'm here, Mother, oh, Mother, I am here.

I had been charming her that long drive long
but she was never superstitious.
That's probably why it didn't work.

Well, after that, we were all very gay
as people are when the worst has happened.
You know how that goes:
The mind dresses itself up

And I thought a lot
About how I never learned one damned thing
From her.
Her mind was narrow
As a string

36

But now
I think of her when I see marshmallows
Something whitens in me and salutes
The sixteen hours that bent chest pushed
its load against all odds.

Stepmother

He married me for my back, you know,
I was stronger than any man he could have hired
and cheaper.

The girls and I—those two sweet lumps of lard—
had lost our bearings: their father died
chopping down a sycamore, one hand to heart
and time enough to call,
but there was nothing we could do.

Your father went as quickly but
no neighbors came to help.
I cleaned him up myself (that one old suit)
and in a makeshift box—part chicken coop—
and dug a shallow grave. Four feet, the best
that I could do, behind the shed and on that little knoll
beside her. Then etched his name "John" over "Ella"
stark as pain on the crude stone.

Look at my hands.
When we met, your father
took my hand and dropped it,
shocked at skin as rough as barn plank.
"Marry me?"
Of course. I had few options.
We joined the two small farms and made a living,
digging sprouts to clear the land to plant the corn
to sell in town to buy the flour, tea, and oil for lamps—
whatever we could not coax from the land.

You were eleven then—frail as the teacups
in her room he never let me touch.
We worked our days—the girls beside me, humble
as the gentlest cow,

until the sun went down.
They helped me with the supper for five of us to share.

You nibbled like a mouse.
My two great girls wolfed down their food:
the greens, potatoes, ham, and bread.
Tea with honey—
sometimes, feeling grand.

Oh, we had plenty.
There was no lack of food.
What I missed—I'm hungry even now—
was touch, I think, or look, some spirit food,
something warm and sweet and humming.
God, how I longed for love!

But what he knew of tenderness
he kept for you.
Brushing that spun gold hair,
crooning like a lover.

And her.
Night after night he closed himself inside her room.
For what? I never knew.
Perhaps to contemplate and to compare
that precious hothouse flower
with the old work mule he toiled beside.

He never touched me.
Once, bringing in the hay,
our shoulders brushed.
You would have thought I'd kicked him.
His lips curled and he spat,
yes, spat on the ground beside my shoe.

I was not her, you see.
Ella. Probably he called it in his sleep;
I was not close enough to hear.
I won't say there was no pleasure in it—
these past five years:
wild roses thick around the nearest pasture;
those jars of jams and pickles gleaming on the shelf;
crocks of milk cooling in the cellar.
A good day's work can shine like polished silver.

At night, the bed's sweet comfort—
lonely though it was—
received my tired, old bones.
I went to sleep to whippoorwills.

Since he died, you've crouched there by the fire,
dabbling in the ashes.
But don't you see? The work goes on.
That one peach tree needs pruning
and cows need milking twice a day.

And you. You feed your face—that heart-shaped face—
at the table I provide;
your clothes no worse than mine
but not as clean;
yet the same shaded creek in which I wash my dress
runs clear for you as well.

Am I bitter? I have the sadness all ugly women have.
"Ugly as a mud fence," my mother used to say,
herself lovely as a tulip.
Even my first husband on our wedding day
said his vows and looked away
though I was young then,
young and thin.

40

And now it's come to this.
No effort of your own
but Lady Luck has smiled on you
and smiled and smiled
in spangles, jewels, silks, and furs
and handsome princes dancing.
Princess. Queen.
Lovely as spring flowers, violets perhaps.
Yes. Moist violets peeping through a late March snow.

Oh, I was never blind to beauty—
in nature, you, or anyone.

I never beat you; never banished you to hearth or room.
But I have envied—how I have—
that fine gold hair your father loved;
that skin like cream and roses;
eyes blue as your mother's china.
And feet? Feet small as mice
with matching set of hands.

I ask for nothing now.
Only that you try to understand.
When the horse—white as curd—
stops at our humble door
and you ride off to arms that cherish,
hands that tangle in your hair,
ask yourself what you have done
to earn such fortune.
Why you and not another,
my own dear, docile Sweets perhaps?

41

It's planting time. Come sunrise
the girls and I will hitch the mare to plow first garden.
The plowpoint, sharpened with an arrowhead,
will slice the earth as neat as glass,
glass cut for tiny slippers.

By harvest time, some man—no prince on stallion—
but tired and needing help with canning
will come riding here with modest hope.

And that's all right
I have learned to handle that.

Landing

We bent over backwards to re-wind the years
as if we knew we were evolving, shedding
some invisible membrane we were reluctant
to let go.

We have always been too cerebral.

Were we trying to freeze-frame some process
like those cameras aimed at flowers
to catch nature in its act?

Or were we hoping some nubbin-like
new beginning might yet emerge and surprise us?

God, we were restless and so frightened.
Not of each other.

Dark (clockwise and obedient)
made a smooth and noiseless landing.

It was time, we knew, to unbuckle.

Such heavy luggage on the carousel—
the kind that has no music.

How much pretense is involved here?

I think not much.

Between us two, metaphor may be the only thing
we understand.

The Combination

Touching my knobs and buttons
with practiced hands
you dial your favorite response.

A creak in the heating
and you must begin again
turning, pressing, pushing
the old combination

as familiar and unconscious
as the act of breathing
and no less dear.

What Did You See?

when you looked past the momentous and momentary
pleasure
his body all over and around as the atmosphere

those vows, stronger than love, that took him back
whether he willed or not?

What did you see?

Did your arms feel only the place he had been
empty even as he filled it?

Or his muscle memory enfolding your shape, your design
as it fought to remember mine?

To be with him with me
after all
is that some consolation?

Tongue-tied

I never told you
I once saw
strolling with your father
around a winter pond
ducks planted white on white.

This is my love letter.
Read between its lines.
It's the only one I'll write.

Guilt Before Dawn

The morning hasn't started yet.
Little ones folded into sleep
are still
or in dozing mode
they rest their tiny bones
just as well
good as sleep.

All quiet on the inside
quiet as a dead baby's throat.

The air—wind actually—
prowls meanly
lights on a robin egg
half outside its webbed cradle
nudges it down
to the passive ground
to a baby blue splash
no louder than dimples on the sun.

Some say:
        Christ died on the cross
        for you and you
        your sins
        dark and ugly
        dark and bloody
        on the cross.

Some, alert at this hour, say:
        no broken egg,
        however pretty
        no flesh raptured by pain
        can atone
        can even matter.

Arms

When you closed your face
and turned your back on me,
I held out my arms and
stretched and stretched
until my arms grew thin as string
to pull you home.

But you were gone
locked behind some private wound
where memory's cold metallic spoon
blends miffs and actual wrongs,
puts out the Closed Forever sign.

Only in dreams I hold you still,
Still as a corpse all color gone.
But I cannot let go!
Broken hearts can only hum.
Mine will forever hum a lullaby.

They Brought Food

Such loud-mouthed food
I could hear it babbling from every room
in the house.

Mounds and mounds of chicken with the hearts
still beating beside the lady like asparagus
and hearty laugh of the jumbo rolls
and lively tunes of the casseroles.

In the attic where I went looking for relief
the food song whistled through the vents,
sang through the ceiling cracks: jellied shapes
and pasta salads chanting: "Eat. Eat."

And we ate. We ate like animals home with our kill.
We formed a circle, licked our palms, wiped our fingers
in our hair. Such streams of colorful juices leaked
from our mouths, formed rainbows at our feet.

Our stomachs full, we stuffed our heads
our arms and legs so not one breath,
one hair of space was left,
not a seam, not a crack.

And still it came: blow after blow of suffocating pain.
It hit us with our mouths wide open
sucking air and blood and butterscotch.

Our eyes bulged—wild strawberries on a sea of foam...
There were knives of celery sharp in our hearts
stabbing, stabbing the message that
no matter how we gorged and gorged
we could not cure the world of dying
nor find the place where we begin
since you left off.

49

Better Closing Lines

(For Jim Wayne Miller)

Poems help, of course, and music—Mozart
and maybe Patsy Cline;
a hymn my preacher (read *Actor*) father sang
or danced "Some glad morning when this life is o'er";
and memories.

Remembering: that time we danced to radio around the living room.
My hurt heart made my body stiff at first,
but when my stroked bones softened,
"Ah, ahh, God," you said.
You knew then that I would take you back.
And when I whispered, "In sickness and in health,"
oh, how you cried.

There's darkness now. I dance alone
in your old shirt and hold your photograph.
"I go out walkin' after midnight."
At other times, I tremble, squeal in terror
like a cornered, unarmed rat.

Where are you now, my gentle dancing boy,
young in my mind as the day we met?
There was such sweetness in you on your mother's side
Those lips sweet as images in country music songs.
Fingers stuffed like sausages with promise.
Dear God, I love you so.

Remembering that (on the other hand):
you were built somewhat odd.
It can be hard to forgive a thing like that.

Shape. Shape. It's shape I missed.
I was annoyed by the flabby, formless nature of it all.

50

No climax, denouement.
Only the steady noise of our little box-shaped friend,
A sturdy little soldier, full of purpose,
kind as a saint.

Still, for protocol, there was your mother.
Stiff-lipped and deferential.
With awful pride, she said,
"He closed his eyes; he closed his eyes."
I had not known that that's a deathbed test.

And so you passed, my darling,
passed.

Our little band, neat as a package,
wrapped around your narrow, rented bed.
And how relieved they were that I—
my father's daughter—starved for theater,
begging then and now for better closing lines—
"When I die, hallelujah, by-and-by—"
ruined, blasted wild with grief,
a circling bird with half a heart,
allowed myself a modest,
"Go with God, Baby.
Go with God."

At Your Grave: Some Random Thoughts

I like to believe
they treated your body
with care
with respect
you never gave it;

that your veins are now roads
for all kinds of underground
life—teeming and vibrant—

that bustles along
at this very moment
delivering tiny dots of food
to tinier mouths

while your grave proudly
holds up your very own stone:
the one thing on this earth
indisputably yours:
a name tag, a death tag

reflecting the sun in little
rays almost invisible
but sure as the grass
that grows brown
then green again

at some private command
that cannot be resisted
as the wind tells the chimes
I hung on your dogwood tree,
"Sing! Sing!"

Butterscotch

After you died, I blundered on as best I could
with the urgencies of living:

There's a pork roast dressed in fresh sage
doing its thing in the oven;

I have made Grandmother's butterscotch pie—
butter, brown sugar, a lost art really;

and her coleslaw that dates back to pre-mayonnaise—
cabbage tossed in vinegar sweetened with sugar.

The whole world as everyone knows is one big old ball
of a metaphor, so anything goes—

pie works as well as sky
if you think about it.

Well, I had to find some way to go on living
which is not the same thing as finding a reason

and so I returned to the ways of my people—
pale, nervous citizens who dwell in the hills

under aprons of trees in perpetual shadows.
They praise the Lord nightly for all of their blessings.

They know how to feast on cold pork and leftover pie.
They touch me ever so shyly.

Their kind eyes brush me with love:
"Have some more, Child."

53

They will save my soul if I let them:
"Jesus loves you."

Yes, I know.
This is my home.
These are my people.

Afterword

Mary Ellen Miller's stunning volume gathers the elements of a woman's full cosmology in poems that are fierce, elegant, and intelligent. In ode-like, elastic forms, Miller takes us into the dark frolic of the family, the world, and a woman's quest to secure the ascendancy of the creative self.

These poems offer us the steady gaze into the dazzling and sometimes deadly mire of the trauma, both private and public. Her language is charged with emotional pulsations that are gathered, seized and released into bold figurative gestures before their secrets can be spoiled or dishonored by mere discourse.

In *The Poet's Wife Speaks* we enter a life lived in close proximity to the wound as well as the joys that matter and endure. Can poetry make sense of our ontological traumas and dilemmas? Might art help us survive?

For Mary Ellen Miller, the poet is a gatherer of imperfections that are transformed into jewels— poems with dangerous interiors brewing within civil forms of elegant, heart-breaking restraint.

Dwell long enough in these poems and you may discover the urgencies of Miller's quiet credo: "Now you know why—some of the time—I love the world and all that's in it."
In this bold and generous gathering of poems, we might well continue answering Virginia Woolf's provocation, "…who shall measure the heat and

violence of the poet's heart when caught in a woman's body?"

George Eklund
Morehead State University

About the Author

Mary Ellen Miller is Professor of English at Western Kentucky University, where she teaches American Literature, Creative Writing, and general education courses.

She has published essays, articles, reviews, and poetry, but *The Poet's Wife Speaks* is her first book of poems. In the 1980's, she and co-producer Michael Lasater won the Red Ribbon Award at the New York Film Festival for their documentary, *Poetry: A Beginner's Guide.*

Prof. Miller and co-editor, Dr. Morris Grubbs of the University of Kentucky are currently working on a collection of the poems, fiction, and essays of Jim Wayne Miller.

The collection, *A Jim Wayne Miller Reader*, will be published by the University Press of Kentucky.

Made in the USA
Middletown, DE
15 October 2018